SMART LITTLE ME!

LYNETTE ALLI

To order additional copies of this book, contact:
Xlibris
1-888-795-4274
www.Xlibris.com
Orders@Xlibris.com

This Book deals with readiness of Infants,
and Toddlers to identify themselves.

Smart   Little   ME!

Sincere thanks to my husband, Akbar,
daughter, Nezie and son-in-law, Raymond,
for their help and support.

insert toddler's photo here

Hello! this is ME.

My name is _____.

I am a little child.

I am ready to learn all about me.

I want to know you, and more about me.

I have two bright little eyes.

I can see you, and you can see me.

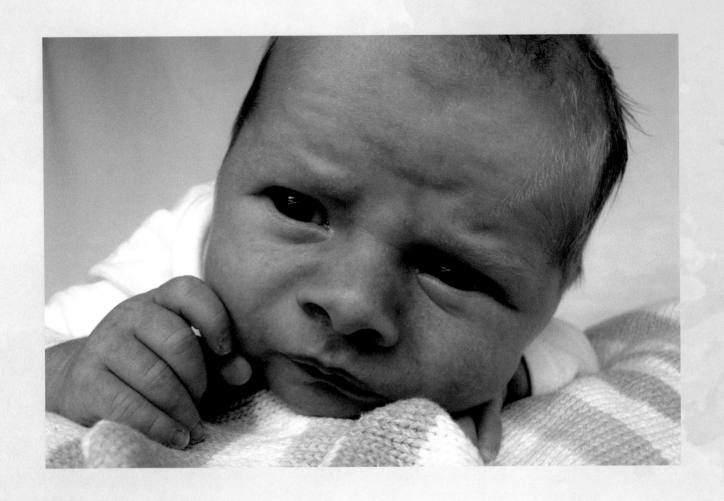

I have a dear little nose.

I can smell with my dear little nose.

I can smell something with my dear little nose.

Something smells really good.

I have two tiny ears.

I can hear with my tiny ears.

I can hear you say, "love you."

I can hear you singing, "la la, la la"

You can hear me saying, "mom, mom, and da da."

I have a cute little mouth.

I can smile with you, when you smile with me.

I have two small hands.

I have a right hand, and I have a left hand.

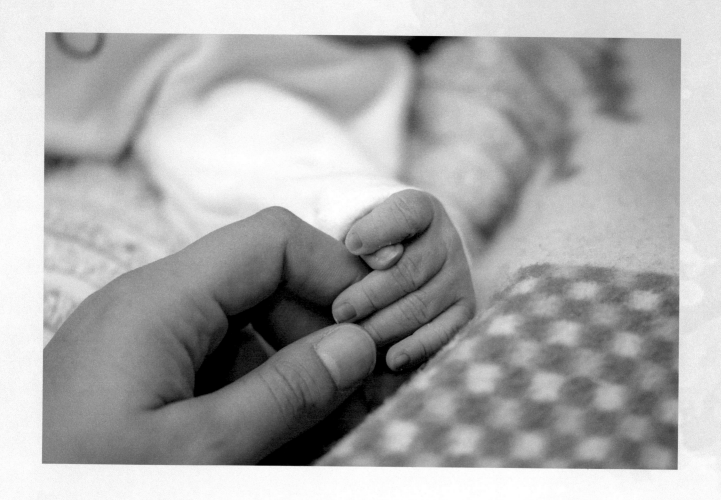

I can hold your hand with my small little hand.

I have two strong little feet.

I have a right foot, and I have a left foot.

I can stand straight, and tall with
my strong little feet.

I have ten lovely fingers.

I can count my fingers with you.

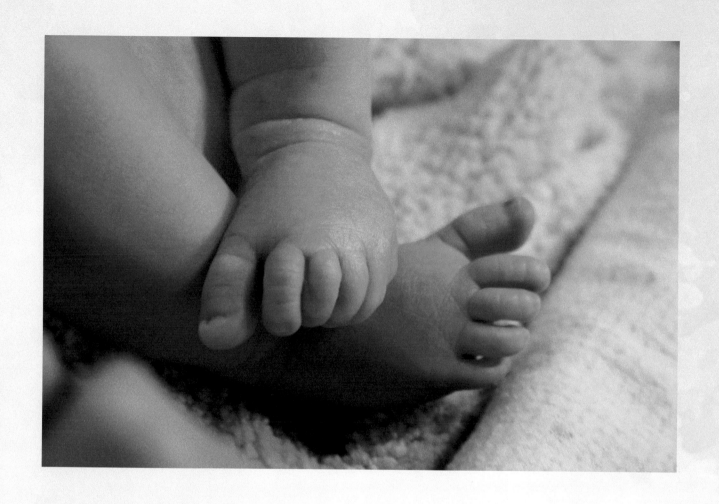

I have ten nice little toes.

I can count my toes with you.

Now I know all about me, and all about you.

It's me, smart little ME!

Hello! It's me, smart little ME!

Printed in the United States
By Bookmasters